Epoxy Epistles

Letters That Stick

Thomas D. Peterson

C.S.S. Publishing Co., Inc.
Lima, Ohio

EPOXY EPISTLES

Library of Congress Cataloging-in-Publication Data

Peterson, Thomas D.
Epoxy epistles.

1. Church bulletins. I. Title.
BV653.3.P47 1987 254.4 86-28355
ISBN 0-89536-868-4

7827 / ISBN 0-89536-868-4 PRINTED IN U.S.A.

Table of Contents

In Memoriam

Eleanor Mary Magdalene Martin

To

Lynn and Bruce
Tom and Linda

Who help make up the Epoxy of my life

Preface

Dear Brother, Sister Pastor,

I look back over the many letters I have written in my church newsletters, and I cringe. I read letters I receive in newsletters from other pastors, and, more often than not, I cringe.

Too often our letters are commentaries on the changing seasons. "Here it is September again — time to get back — had a rest — ready to dig in — happy fellowship lies ahead." "Well, what do you know, it's Thanksgiving already — harvest — plenty — why not be thankful." "My, how time flies. It's spring . . . soon. Lent — lengthen — spring — new life — my goodness how wonderful it all is."

I moved into a new church and happened at that time to see a book of riddles and jokes my wife was previewing for her elementary library, *How Do You Get A Horse Out of the Bathtub?* by Louis Phillips (New York, Viking Press, 1983) Though written for children, most items, after the initial grin of recognition, leave a lot left over for speculation.

I started using them to prime my thoughts. People began to say they looked forward to them. I'm in hopes the result might stimulate the reader to fresh and pertinent material for parish letters.

Yours,

Thomas D. Peterson

(All Question and Answer quotations are from Phillips, pp. 1-22)

Foreword

Monday morning can be a let-down for any minister after a rewarding or hectic Sunday. The spark of inspiration for the "Pastor's Corner" in the newsletter or the regular epistle to persons of the congregation may be missing. If Thomas Peterson's collection of letters doesn't directly stimulate a theme for the weekly message, a new idea will spin itself out in unexpected ways.

The first letter in the following collection is a clue about the author. His "thing" is deep reflection without being dull — in fact, it is depth inspired by humor. These teasingly funny quips lead into some profound comments.

The letters also reveal the author's faith in human potential — potential to discover the spirit of God within, to use God-given intelligence, to trust, to love, to recognize mystery, to be courageous, and even to be appropriately humble. At the same time, the letters show the love and support of a minister for his people, a model for every Christian community.

Don't miss the "sign off" phrases which, in selected letters, give an extra kick, like "yours for turning," "yours for a safe journey home," and many more.

If you are stuck without the foggiest notion of what to write in your column, these "letters that stick" fling loose fresh ideas in a mood of laughter and hope.

T. William Hall
Emeritus Professor of Religion
Syracuse University

1

Dear Friend,

Q: "I'm thinking of studying oceanography. Can you tell me what qualities are needed by a good oceanographer?"

A: "An oceanographer is a person who likes to *explore things in depth!*"*

I'm looking for people to specialize in a unique field. After the definition above, I've decided we need lots of them. A lot of "oceanographic" activities are going on at ________ Church this coming year. Wanted: Enthusiastic oceanographers!

Yours,

(Suggested use: First week of church program year)
*Phillips, p. 7.

2

Dear Friend,

Q: "Two years ago my parents gave me a camera for Christmas. Since then, I've taken thousands of pictures. If I sent you some of my photos, could you tell me if they are any good?"

A: "Sorry, but I refuse to make 'snap' judgments."*

Two thousand years ago God gave the world a moving picture of himself, Jesus. Like all movies it is made up of thousands of "snaps." Each is important; but, all together, they tell the Story. Too often we make judgments about the Gospel from just a few "snaps."

It's the same with people we meet. They are moving pictures. Nevertheless, we persist in making judgments from a few "snaps." Unfortunately, we are the losers, for the deep riches of the person escape us. All prejudice comes under the heading of "snap" judgment. We do not bother to look at the whole picture and see what is really at work.

Lord, help us to avoid making snap judgments. There is more to each of us than meets the eye at first glance. Inside us all are marvelous wonders we could easily miss if we go by snap judgments. Help us to look and see!

Yours,

Phillips, p. 3.

3

Dear Friend,

I recently came across the Chinese character printed below. The meaning of it struck me, and I thought you would find significance in it, too. This is the written form of *xin,* which is the rough equivalent of "fidelity" in English. "Fidelity" is the quality of being faithful, dependable, reliable. The character depicts a man (left) standing by his word (right). To stand by one's word, to let the *yes* be *yes* and the *no* be *no,* is to be dependable. We might say that such a person's word is his bond. Such fidelity to one's word gives a man or woman a space in which he or she can stand.

Yours for a Chinese character,

4

Dear Friend,

Q: "My grandparents gave me a dog for my birthday. Unfortunately, my dog has no ears. What should I call it?"

A: "There's no sense in calling it anything, since it won't hear you anyway!"*

Roughly 2500 years ago God used this idea when he called Isaiah. There will always be people who "hear, but don't hear," or "see, but don't see." Or, in other words, people who hear, but do not understand, and see, but do not perceive. (Isaiah 6:9ff)

Jesus knew the Scripture. He knew there are times when people can hear, and times when they can't. He even talked as if they might not have ears, just as in the joke above: "He who has ears to hear, let him hear . . ." (Matthew 11:15), or to paraphrase "If you have ears, listen!"

There are times when life goes so smoothly that we in effect "don't have ears" — we have no need to hear anything beyond what we're immediately involved in. But there are other times when we need to acquire ears rapidly, because there are things going on that we want to tune in to. Our lives demand involvement, *action!* At these times, we must be on the alert, pray deeply, carefully study God's Word, listen intently to those who have something to say, and tune in to those deep mysteries of life and of the spirit we are just beginning to "hear."

Yours,

*Phillips, p. 2.

5

Dear Friend,

Q: "I have a bad cold. My father says that I should drink a large glass of carrot juice after a hot bath. What do you think?"

A: "I think that after you drink the hot bath, you will not have any room for the carrot juice!"*

Life is like that. When we are busy with large things we do not have room for little things. For instance, when we are constructively employed we do not have time for mischief. When we are busy giving ourselves away, we don't have room in our hearts to be miserly. When we take charge of our own health, we do not have room for excess smoking, drinking, or junk foods.

In short, when we are busy being *big* we do not have room in our lives to be *little.* When we are full of Christ, we no longer have room to house resentment, fear, anger, or grudge. Lots of gnawing, fretful, limiting things that distort our lives cannot find room when he is in our hearts. Our fervent prayer is for Christ to be Chief guest in our hearts. When he is present, we won't have room for activities and attitudes we really dislike about ourselves.

Yours for an important Guest,

*Phillips, p. 2

6

Dear Friend,

Q: "My psychiatrist says that I am suffering from kleptomania. What should I do?"

A: "Whatever you do, don't take anything for it!"*

Believe it or not, there are times in life when to do nothing is better than to do something. "I'm suffering from greed. What should I do?" "Whatever you do, don't take anything for it!" The greedy person feels that one more acquisition, and, then, the process can stop. But, no, by doing nothing the circle of greed is cut, and the problem is stopped dead in its tracks.

I'm suffering from anger. What should I do?" "Whatever you do, don't get mad about it!" The tendency is to go and tell whomever off. Get the record straight; let 'em know just how dastardly they treated you, how unfair life has been. Then, when it is out of your system, you will be purged of anger. But one mad-on added to another is like another log on the fire and merely heats up the process. What is needed in life is the art of cutting the circle before it grows so tight it strangles.

Can this apply to you? Have you been too hard on yourself? If you're under too much pressure, don't complicate it by adding any more to your burden than you absolutely need to carry. Don't "take anything for it!" Isaiah 30:15 says it well: "In returning and rest shall ye be saved; in quietness and in trust shall be your strength." Freedom to be at peace alone with God is often the best medicine.

Yours,

*Phillips, p.4

7

Dear Friend,

Look at the ships also; though they are so great and are driven by strong winds, they are guided by a very small rudder wherever the will of the pilot directs. (James 3:4)

The mental picture James gives us would be humorous if it were not destructive. A ship on a great ocean in strong winds — like a chip floating down a great river — yet the pilot guides it as he wills without regard to the storm!

We all do this in some way or other. My mother used to say to me, "You'd cut off your nose to spite your face." Folk sayings have a way of cutting through a subject to its very heart.

Many forces in life move us whether we will or not — accidents, natural events, the actions of others. We have no choice but to move along in the direction they set for us. But in our ships we have control over the rudder that guides us. We are in charge of the will by which we direct our lives. So even when buffeted by the overwhelming forces of life, we can adapt to these forces, learn from them, or persist in running against overwhelming strong winds.

What ultimately matters is not so much what happens to a person, as the kind of person it happens to. Whatever our situation, God calls us to take charge of the course of our lives, guiding our ship to port in accordance with the strong winds with which he surrounds us.

Yours,

8

Dear Friend,

Q: "I think I'm losing my memory. What should I do?"

A: "Try to forget about the problem."*

I have an aunt who, every time she starts feeling sorry for herself, buys a small gift and visits someone. She forgets about her problem in reaching beyond herself. I find in my own life that forgiving is a way of forgetting. I forget by forgiving, and not the other way around. How about you?

The above is not bad counsel. There's a great deal to say for hunting out a problem, understanding why it exists, and then freeing yourself from it so you can get on with your journey. *But,* there's also a lot to say about letting the problem be while you move out and do something new and exciting. Often, when you get back to the problem, you will find it is not as difficult as you had thought.

Moving out is a way of moving on, of continuing your journey, of quitting feeling sorry for yourself, of forgetting and forgiving, of doing something constructive with your lives. So this week my wish to you is:

Try a little forgetfulness!

Yours,

*Phillips, p. 4.

9

Dear Friend,

"As a door turns on its hinges, so does a sluggard on his bed." (Proverbs 26:14)

Have you ever waked up to the sound of "bang . . . bang . . . bang-BANG!" at night, only to discover that the outside door had not been closed tightly and was swinging in every gust of wind? Without a will of its own, the door helplessly responded to whatever force hit it.

So it is with the sluggard who turns on his or her bed according to first this whim and then that. Every least feeling or thought stirs to motion, but this motion is quickly changed with the next whim.

Jesus had a pertinent comment on this type of behavior. "Could you not watch with me one hour?" he asked his disciples in Gethsemane. (Mark 14:37) Without this least loyalty, a commitment to one hour, there is very little prospect that a disciple will become a faithful servant.

So it is with us. Somewhere deep within ourselves there must be some strength, some glue that holds us to a good thought, a noble intent — long enough that we begin to understand what it means. Then, it is that our will can turn our lives around and we begin to do the good that we would.

Yours for turning,

10

Dear Friend,

Q: "For the past eight months I've been suffering from insomnia. Do you think my problem is serious?"

A: "Well, I wouldn't lose any sleep over it!"*

This rather corny little joke creeps up on us and packs a wallop. "For the past eight months I've been suffering from cowardice. Do you think my problem is serious?" "Well, I wouldn't lose any courage over it!"

The applications go on and on. When worried about our health, we would not want to lose health over it. When worried about our family we wouldn't want to lose our family over it. When worried about the state of our souls, we wouldn't want to lose our relationship to Jesus over it.

There is a point in life when worrying about our problem makes it worse. Practical action must begin. We quit worrying about our health and begin to do what we already know about maintaining good health. We quit worrying about the state of our family and begin to enrich and enjoy the one we have. We quit worrying about our souls and do the things that keep relationship with Jesus.

The more frantic we become over a problem the less likely we are to do constructive things about it. Without a bit of moving-out courage, it is hard to get off dead center.

Yours for moving-out,

*Phillips, p. 3.

11

Dear Friend,

Q: "I am a teacher of astronomy, but fewer and fewer students are signing up for my course. Why do you think fewer people than ever before are studying astronomy?"

A: "Because the subject is over most people's heads."*

It's funny — a lot of people avoid studying a subject they feel is over their heads. But if you think about it, the very fact that a subject is difficult is an excellent reason to study it! If we already know everything about a subject — if it is only at head level — there is no need for study. The motivation for serious mental stretching comes when a subject *is* over the student's head. And once we begin, with the help of a competent teacher we may discover there are stars up there!

The same lesson can be applied to the Bible. Why does it seem that fewer and fewer people are willing to undertake a study of the Bible? Because they feel the subject is over their heads. A lifelong agenda is required for the wisest person to come to a working understanding of God's ways. So the average person, faced with the prospect of real mental stretching, turns away.

Consider taking the opposite course: get your head up there in the clouds; into the mystery of God's ways with us; into the history of his relations with humankind; into the stars and the firmament he created. Through such efforts you will come to know better the Son whom he made like us, so that we might have a better chance of grasping his wondrous ways.

Yours in reaching for the stars,

*Phillips, p. 20

12

Dear Friend,

Set up waymarks for yourself, make yourself guideposts; consider well the highway, the road by which you went. Return, O virgin Israel, return to these your cities. (Jeremiah 31:21)

The word "guideposts," title of a popular magazine, has become a household word. I had always thought the term originated with the magazine. To my happy surprise I chanced upon this verse, ". . . make yourself guideposts."

The Israelites knew the desert highway by which they were taken into exile. They had passed certain valleys, skirted unique mountains, walked over dry river beds, and made their way over passes. In their minds' eye they could retrace their journey, considering well the road by which they went, and thus set up guideposts so that when the time came to return they could find their way safely home.

The journey back to the Promised Land is actually a metaphor for living. We are encouraged to look back and review the route by which we came to despair — "consider well the highway." We can note the obstinate acts, the stubbornness of will that caused us to persist in a destructive course, and the misuse of others to bolster our sagging egos. Put up guideposts! On the way back to sanity and mental health we will be able to avoid, skirt, pass over, and circle around those self-imposed obstacles that stand in the way of a safe return home.

Do not miss the insight this verse gives. God has vested enough intelligence and moral power in each of us to enable us to gain an understanding of how we got into our predicament and to chart guideposts for a safe return to our rightful place in life.

Yours for a safe journey home,

13

Dear Friend,

John 3:16 is the gospel in a nutshell: "For God so loved the world that he gave his only Son, that whoever believes in him should not perish but have eternal life." But my favorite verse is the one that follows: "For God sent the Son into the world, not to condemn the world, but that the world might be saved through him."

Some sermons stick in the mind for years. I once heard a preacher speak of the passion some religious groups have for the end of the world. Considering how God loved his creation and held it to be good, he could not accept that God is in a hurry to destroy it. Rather, God is always at work trying to save the world. Otherwise, how could his beloved people live constructively in a world that was inherently evil and deserving of destruction?

John 3:17 is the tree on which the nutshell gospel grows. In Jesus, God himself was incarnate in flesh, giving honor to the flesh even as God honored his works in the very act of creating them. The world is the proving ground in which human life, embodied in mortal flesh, briefly works out its service to God.

As surely as the second verse follows the first, so does the meaning of the first lead inevitably to the second. To believe is not an act of the mind apart from action of life. Those who believe cease to condemn the world, for we are in effect condemning God's commitment in Christ Jesus. Instead, we become co-saviors of it. Our task: to see the merit in the world which prompted God's willingness to become incarnate in Jesus.

Yours,

14

Dear Friend,

"I press on toward the goal for the prize of the upward call of God in Christ Jesus . . . I do not consider that I have made it my own . . . forgetting what lies behind . . . straining forward to what lies ahead . . . Let those of us who are mature be thus minded." (Philippians 3:12-15)

Among the many characteristics I received from my parents, two in particular come to mind when I read this passage. My father had a simple but profound way of paying a man a compliment. "Mr. _______ is a man," he would say. An entire mystique was built into his statement, and I still respond to it. When I want to bestow high praise on another male, I hark back to my father's statement. Likewise, a praiseworthy woman was a "lady." This, too, was an ultimate compliment and encompassed an entire battery of desirable traits.

Another legacy was not so helpful. I was taught to respect adults for no other reason than that they were farther along in years than I. It was "Yes, Sir; No, Ma'am," no matter what the situation. I simply assumed that an accumulation of years constituted grounds for wisdom, or at least the privilege of deference. A major lesson in my life has been to come to terms with what maturity really is.

Now you can understand why this passage of Scripture strikes me with such force. Those who are mature have a goal to strive for; they move upward toward Christ; they are not self-centered; they put aside what is past; and they move ever forward to what the future offers. The accumulation of years hardly enters Paul's picture of the mature person.

The upward call of God in Christ Jesus is the condition for genuine maturity.

Yours in pressing upward,

15

Dear Friend,

Q: "What is propaganda?"

A: "Propaganda is a socially correct duck."*

I like this riddle. It creeps up on me and tickles my funny-bone. Naturally it sets me to thinking. What other words can we play with? "Propagate" is such a word. It means "to cause to continue, carry forward, transmit." We propagate our fortunes, the family line, the faith.

A propagate is an acceptable entrance.

There are many places we long to be and situations we long to enjoy. We long for a good position and desire good friends. What are the "acceptable entrances" by which we move into these longings? Let's see: education, experience, industry are "acceptable entrances" to good positions. And, attention to others, respect, and care for their concerns are "proper gates" to friendship.

We also long to enter into a saving relationship with Christ. What is the "proper gate"? Readiness to hear his word, openness to change, and experimentation with his teachings — these provide an "acceptable entrance" to a growing relationship with him.

No one need tell us what gates we wish to enter. We long for them constantly and day-dream about them continuously. What we might need is to be reminded of what gates are proper to enter into what we desire. With the few suggestions given above we can make many a grand entrance!

Yours,

*Phillips, p. 17.

16

Dear Friend,

Everyday language has many phrases that sound wise and promise good prospects. For instance, "cooking on the back burner," sounds as if a major project is boiling away and will soon be ready to eat. Politicians like "make hard choices" and "establish priorities," phrases that hold out prospects for courageous decision and sound solutions. Alas, we all know such are not really meant; rather, action is shunted aside. The promise disappears on examination.

The Christian faith is not without its mirage-words. "As much faith as the next person" is a prime example. Or, "I don't know where I would be without prayer," uttered unctuously. Or what about, "I'm all in favor of religion, but you don't have to be a fanatic." These phrases are like mirages, floating vaguely in the haze of the mind, giving an illusion of substance, but evaporating as soon as we come close. They make us feel devout, but, when analyzed, the true meaning eludes us as the mist does the morning sun.

A woman came to her pastor. She was in great distress and repeated several times that she could not live without her faith. Since, by her own admission, her life was crumbling, the pastor encouraged her to set to work to bolster the faith she had. He suggested regular worship, Bible study, and volunteer service. She sat up abruptly. "Well, I don't mean that I want to be at church every time the door opens. I don't have time for that." So carried away was she with her mirage-words that when serious challenge came she recoiled in alarm.

Watch out for mirage-words that obscure relationship with Christ and keep us from truly getting to know him.

Yours,

17

Dear Friend,

Q: "What word is made shorter by adding a syllable to it?"

A: "Short."*

By adding this same syllable to many words we radically alter their meaning. Love becomes lover; care, carer; help, helper; doubt, doubter; belief, believer. We move from a concept to everyday life. We move from a general idea to specific fact — you . . . me.

We can talk elegantly and feel nobly about love, but without being a lover we know little about it in truth. The magic syllable moves an ethereal notion to the everyday living reality of me and you.

By adding the transforming syllable we signify something very important to those around us and the world. "Here I come." However poor a lover or carer I am, I'm me and I'm loving and caring. I've changed radically from merely thinking or talking about it. I'm real and serious about being a lover, carer, doubter, believer, helper! Watch out world! *Here I come!*

Yours,

*Phillips, p. 16.

18

Dear Friend,

"For he who finds me finds life and obtains favor from the Lord; but he who misses me injures himself; all who hate me love death." (Proverbs 8:35-36)

My mother used to say to me, often, "You'd cut off your nose to spite your face." At last I figured it out. She meant that I was a willful young person and would persist in my own way even if it injured me.

If a person persists in his own way even to the point of self-injury, is this not a little like choosing death? This might seem extreme to you. After all, isn't it human nature to want your own way, and where would we be if people didn't persist?

Ok, I can accept that. But, what about when a person keeps on persisting and persisting when the evidence is to the contrary? To injure oneself time after time and never be willing to look and see what's happening is a path that leads to less life. Less life is death.

Might it be true that we injure ourselves because we have missed God. We have chosen ourselves and persist in choosing ourselves no matter what.

Try God, "For he who finds God finds life and obtains favor from the Lord."

Yours for a good-looking face,

19

Dear Friend,

Why is gossip like a photograph? It comes from something negative that has been developed and enlarged.

Scripture has denounced gossip from the beginning. The Levitical Laws include this one, "Don't gossip. Don't falsely accuse your neighbor of some crime, for I am Jehovah." (Leviticus 19:16, *The Living Bible*) The Ten Commandments makes it loud and clear, "Neither shall you bear false witness against your neighbor." (Deuteronomy 5:20)

False witness is nothing less than gossip. It comes out of making statements of another (a witness to that person) that are not grounded in fact (false).

The church is a gathered community. It lives on a network of trust. To spread false witnesses is to tear apart the community. That which was gathered becomes tattered.

Yours,

20

Dear Friend,

Q: "I understand that an inventor has crossed an electric blanket with an electric toaster. What does his invention accomplish?"

A: "It pops people out of bed in the morings."*

One of the "unforgettable people" I have known was Mrs. O'Hanlon. She was a terrific church person. For several years of my pastorate in her church she was president of the women's work. The first of each month she would phone, asking the number of coffees, luncheons, dinners, etc., the church would need for the month. "Now, don't wait until later to tell me," she would chide. "Tell me now, so I can prepare."

Our phone conversation ended the matter. At the stated day and hour, I would walk into the room and there would be the coffee or the luncheon or whatever was needed.

She once told me how she got her four children to attend church (and they have all become oustanding church persons in their own rights). "I get up early on Sunday morning and make something special for breakfast. When the aroma reaches the kids, they pop out of bed!"

Mrs. O'Hanlon kept lots of things popping. She was a cross between an electric blanket (comforting to those in need), and an electric toaster (getting people to pop up for what they believe). Would that every church could be blessed with a Mrs. O'Hanlon; she was a rare and special breed!

Here's to keeping things popping!,

*Phillips, p. 21.

21

Dear Friend,

"My mouth will speak the praise of the Lord, and let all flesh bless his holy name for ever and ever." (Psalm 145:21)

How does "flesh" bless God's holy name? We are used to blessing God with our hearts, our souls, our minds, our wills — intangible parts of ourselves — but what of flesh, the solid substance in which we walk and talk and move and act in this world?

Flesh blesses God's holy name whenever it gets dressed, walks or drives to church, and takes the heart and will and mind inside to worship. Then, together, they lift up before God a harmony of rejoicing.

Flesh blesses God's holy name when it bends and strives, struggles and rests, and does work. The flesh takes the intentions of the mind and clothes them in useful form to help others. The flesh takes the will and incorporates it in faithful service. The flesh takes the soul and implants it in visible acts of caring.

Flesh blesses God's holy name when it takes a stubborn, prideful will, carries it to the person it has misused, and stands before the offended one until an apology is forthcoming. Flesh collects a paycheck earned with faithful toil and gives a part of it back to do God's work around the world, an act we commonly misattribute to heart and spirit and soul.

Indeed, this verse is an insightful one, reminding us how it is that all things that have breath shall praise the Lord. So, get your flesh moving, united with your heart, mind, will, and soul and "bless his holy name!"

Yours,

22

Dear Friend,

Q: "Why is the sky so high?"

A: "So the birds won't bump their heads."*

Lots of things in this world are so high that no matter how high we fly, we cannot bump our heads against them. Take science, for example: there is no way that anyone can comprehend the full mystery of the natural world. Or art: no one has yet painted the perfect picture, sculpted the perfect statue. Or medicine: despite the most sophisticated medical practices the world has ever seen, we still feel pain and suffer. Even love has its limitations: there are still aches deep within the heart, even though we may love another more than life itself and be so loved in return.

As for following Christ, there have been martyrs, saints, and disciples by the thousands, yet the ultimate life of service has been lived only once.

Each generation has the task of rediscovering life all over again: its unfathomable mystery, its excitement, its loveliness. One might suspect that the world, having progressed so far, is just about to reach perfection. All we need do is read the excessive praise of science and technology and note the absolute faith we have in it. Just a little farther and we will bump our heads on the sky.

Not so! We are rather like the builders of the Tower of Babel. We persist in believing that a little higher and we will be in control of all knowledge and power. Just then the bricks start tumbling down. We find a thing or two we cannot control and a few things we do not know.

We are pilgrims and will always be pilgrims, traveling through a world of mystery and wonder, forever reaching for the sky.

Yours,

*Phillips, p. 21.

23

Dear Friend,

Q: "Can you, in simple terms for the layperson, explain why days are long in the summer and short in the winter?"

A: "Days are long in the summer and short in the winter because heat expands things and cold contracts them!"*

Something in this bit of nonsense reminds me of the church. Why do churches that are hot grow, and churches that are cold shrink? Well, churches that are warm and spirited grow because heat makes them expand, while churches that are cold shrink because cold contracts them!

Have you ever noticed? Warm and congenial, outgoing and responsive congregations have no trouble growing — they are expansive. Churches that are cold and unresponsive, short and curt in manner lose ground because they are retractive.

Studies have shown that people choose a church because the congregation is accepting and welcoming, and not because of the pastor or the choir or other factors. Every person in every church has a unique, distinctive quality of warmth and cordiality to offer.

I love the long, summer-like hours spent in a friendly church, because my heart is warmed. When I leave to go about the business of the week, I feel expansive.

Warmly,

*Phillips, p. 21.

24

Dear Friend,

The female mosquito can fly upside down. What can you do?

I'd like to share some examples from the lives of friends. One, an agoraphobic, was unable to be in crowds, attend group meetings, or function in public settings. She now leads a group of agoraphobics, helping them to take their rightful places in the world. In my opinion, this equals the skill of the female mosquito!

Another friend, loving the Lord and taking seriously his command to visit those in prison, became a highly successful and respected literacy volunteer in a large penitentiary. He moved on in spite of the reservations of the experts and the veiled antagonism buried in the red tape of the bureaucrats. Though a male, he surely outdoes the female mosquito.

There is no telling what you can do! Suppose, hindered by excuses and resentments, you nevertheless find the courage to pry yourself free. Then you go on and do the good you know you should. Against great odds, you enlarge your base of experience and fine-tune your skills. In effect, you are turning your life upside down and moving forward, just like the female mosquito! From then on you can fly free, humming happily and quite unable to bite at the world because, of course, you are flying upside down!

Yours,

25

Dear Friend,

Years ago someone pointed out to me that although other people may be responsible for a problem, I am the only one who can do anything about it. I cannot make another change or behave in a way I think to be fair; but, I can change my own behavior, outlook, or attitude. So the efficient way to get something done is to begin at home.

In *Old First Church,* Earl Jones and Robert L. Wilson (NY, Harper and Row, 1974) researched many formerly prestigious churches which had come upon hard times. Invariably the congregation blamed the pastor, complaining wistfully, "If only we had somebody like Dr. Go Get'm. He filled this church twice every Sunday."

To my surprise, I later came across this same insight in *In Search of Excellence* by Thomas J. Peters and Robert H. Waterman, Jr. (NY, Harper and Row, 1982). The authors were discussing why factories fail. "The failing is often attributed to 'the unions' or 'lack of employee good-will.' Seldom is it attributed to lack of persistence and true caring on the part of management." (p. 241)

Jesus taught us this same lesson: "Why pay attention to the speck in your brother's eye and ignore the log in your own?" (Matthew 7:3) As hard as this lesson may seem, there is happy element in it. No matter the problem, there is something constructive to be done.

You may not be able to make others see their faults or behave in different ways. You can alter your own behavior so as to inject a new element into the situation. You are never without a resource, and that resource is your own willingness to try a new approach.

Yours,

26

Dear Friend,

No wind favors him who has no destined port. (Montaigne)

Some time ago I felt I was suffering from a grave injustice. In fact, I did not merely feel so, I knew so. The time came to confront the parties I held responsible for my ill-treatment. Yet I did not know how to deal with the shame and anger they awakened in me.

Then an idea came to me. "You say Jesus is your Lord and that he enables you to grow almost no matter what. If you choose to cling to your resentment, you cannot have his company. He does not countenance such feelings, no matter how justified. To keep his company, you must let go of such feelings." The wind of injustice and its storm of emotions certainly had blown me off course. I had lost sight of my port. And what was my destined port? What I wanted, more than anything else, was to stay close to Jesus. Once I realized this, the wind that had driven me off course shifted and became one which favored my destination.

So much for the wisdom of Christ that leads us through the storms of life; so much for the power of God that causes all things to work together for good when he is our destined port.

Yours for smooth sailing
and a safe port,

27

Dear Friend,

He who has a "why" to live can bear almost any "how." (Nietzsche)

The husband of a dear friend has Alzheimer's disease in an advanced stage. He no longer knows how to sit down without being guided, is losing his ability to feed himself, and cannot put one word together with another. She cares for him day and night with help from her family. Except for an hour or two a week she never leaves him.

We have just returned from a visit. We look in great sorrow and respect at what we have seen. How does she do it? Her faithfulness surpasses our understanding. Nietzsche gives us an insight. We can grasp "how" she manages because we know "why" she does it in the first place.

She does it because she loves him. She has always loved him. We have witnessed this through thirty years of mutual sacrifice, affection, and devotion given freely.

Why do I always come back from my visit with a confidence that a marvelous force is at work in the world? I feel strongly that, whatever the challenge facing me, there is something important in it which must be won through. I have learned it is not won through by the "how." It is achieved by the "why." In the "why" God shows he has not condemned his world, but is always at work saving it. It is his "why" that helps us make sense out of the confusion, doubt, and uncertainty. After all "God so loved the world . . ."

We live in a world of "how," like the pilot who radioed, "We're making world-record time, but we don't know where we are. God's "why" gives meaning and purpose to all of life.

Yours,

28

Dear Friend,

Q: "My father is working on a collection of quotations from famous people. We would like to know what Thomas Edison said on the day he invented the light bulb."

A: "Edison didn't say a thing. He was too shocked."*

When small things happen to us we find it easy to respond. Someone holds a door. We reply happily "Thank you." A guest gives my wife a hostess gift, and she effuses prettily. Christmas time we bring out all the stops: "Just what I wanted!" "How did you ever . . .?" "This is the most beautiful sweater I've . . .!

When the event is more significant, strangely enough our ability to respond grows, not more, but less: we are aware that whatever we say cannot do justice to the flood of emotion in us. We stumble with words and come out with, "How can I say 'Thank you.'?" Then we squeeze their hand or give a hug to show that our response outruns our ability to show it.

When the gift is unique there is no response. When we are illuminated by a life-saving insight, what can be said? When a blessing of health or privilege comes our way, how can mere words suffice? And, when Christ invites us to be his, a feeling of cosmic import illumines our lives. A major turnaround in our lives changes our world. When Edison was "shocked" his world and ours changed. When we are "shocked" into self-realization in Christ, we have no way to talk about it. Instead we must get busy doing what he compels us to do.

Yours, for the shock of your life,

*Phillips, p. 13.

29

Dear Friend,

As the centuries roll along, the age-old discussion continues: "Do you have to attend church to be a Christian?" Let's take a fresh look at the issue:

Q: "If a group of lions is a pride, and a group of cows a herd, what word is used to describe a group of dermatologists or skin doctors?"

A: "A rash of dermatologists will do nicely."*

What do we call the collected works of a writer: his corpus, the body of his works. When we talk about how people live together, we talk about the corp-orate nature of human society, the body of people at work together. When referring to church members, we use the word "congregation" — those who gather together. A congregation is the coming together of the Body of Christ. Somehow, in some way, we have to gather together to be a Body of Christ, alive and at work in the world.

We still haven't found the answer to our question, but we've come a bit closer. There cannot be a living Body of Christ until we ourselves gather together. What do you call a Christian church? At the least, it is a gathering.

Yours,

*Phillips, p. 12.

30

Dear Friend,

Q: "My little sister watches television sixteen hours a day. Do you think she'll go down in history?"

A: "Not only will she go down in history, but I predict she'll go down in arithmetic, in English, and in geography as well."*

A lesson is here for us all. Too much television, too much leisure time, too much work, too much worry, too much of any given activity to the exclusion of all others, will cause our "marks" to go down all around. Our lives need to be balanced with lots of varied outlets and activities.

We need leisure; we need solitude; but, we also need to take part in the life of the community, in love, in study, in work, in play. Finally, we must glue all the varied aspects of ourselves together with a solid sense of the stewardship of our God-given abilities and talents. Then we won't have to worry about missing out on the wondrous richness that life has to offer.

Even if we don't go down in history, we stand a chance of going down in the memory of our churches and communities!

Yours,

*Phillips, p. 5.

31

Dear Friend,

Q: "I keep getting a ringing in my ears. What should I do?"

A: "Get an unlisted ear!"*

Recently I watched a powerful TV movie about teen suicide. The basic problem, as I saw it, was too many "unlisted ears." "Why didn't I listen? There were so many signals. How could I have not heard?" were the phrases that were repeated time and again.

A major tragedy is not necessary to alert us to the fact that our ears are "unlisted." At the end of each day, we regretfully recall moments we failed to stop and listen to someone we hold dear. And how many times have we ourselves been in distress because those we wished to signal were too preoccupied to hear what we had to say? Then there is the joy of those rare individuals who pay attention to us, take us in, treat us like people who matter simply by listening to what we say. If only we could all be like these!

If you have not taken out a listing in the Celestial Phone Book this year, get in touch quickly and "list" your ears in God's Yellow Pages!

Yours,

*Phillips, p. 8.

32

Dear Friend,

Q: "Do you know of any invention that allows people to see through walls?"

A: "How about windows?"*

"I can see right through you." Knowledge of human nature and sensitivity to other people enable us to see through walls that otherwise would separate us.

"I see a lot of good in her." There is nothing like respect and love to help us see through walls into the goodness which exists in another. Loving is a way of knowing, and knowing allows us to see deeply into the potential of others, past walls and barriers.

"At last I see what you mean." By knocking our heads hard against a problem, trying first this way of looking at it and then that way, we come to see a solution where once there was only a wall.

"I know that of which I am persuaded," goes the statement of faith. And since faith gives us knowledge of "things unseen," we are able to move ahead against almost any odds.

Life gives us many ways to see through walls. There are insight, sensitivity, hard thinking, love, and faith — all allow us to break through what would otherwise be an impenetrable barrier, and make contact with the goodness and truth that exist in all of us.

Yours,

*Phillips, p. 20.

33

Dear Friend,

Q: "Will you please complete the proverb, 'If at first you don't succeed . . .' "

A: "If at first you don't succeed, you should try playing the outfield."*

Did you ever know a spoiled child, used to getting his own way? What happens when he can't have his way? Does he sit back, ponder the situation, and become compliant and obedient? Not by a long shot! He redoubles his efforts, using every trick in his repertoire to get his way.

Did you ever see a person used to winning arguments through anger give up being angry when it's no longer effective? No way. She/he just gets angrier and angrier, determined to have his/her way, no matter what. Most of us, most of the time, have but one string to our guitar. If we don't get the music we desire from one pluck, we pluck that much harder. The world can't get the best of us!

Our mole of a joke contains a mountain of wisdom. If you don't get what you want from one course of action, try another. Try outfield, try first base, try water polo — anything except what is not working. How much grief and pain could be avoided if people would just sit back, reflect, and look around for other means of action. Maybe, just maybe, the method you're trying is the wrong one, and it cannot work, no matter how hard you try.

I'm reminded of a statement you hear often: "After all, I'm doing the best I know how." Yes, you may be doing your best, but your know-how is off base. Try the outfield!

Yours,

*Phillips, p. 14.

34

Dear Friend,

Q: "I love the story of Robin Hood, but can you please tell me why he stole from the rich?"

A: "He stole from the rich because the poor didn't have any money!"*

Two points about being poor: 1. The poor don't have anything, so there is nothing to steal. 2. Since they don't have anything, whatever comes along represents an improvement. In short, the poor have nothing to lose and everything to gain.

The Beatitudes teach us that God blesses the poor in spirit. Keeping in mind that "rich" and "poor" are terms that apply in other matters besides money, perhaps the story of Robin Hood helps us gain new insight into this teaching. The poor in spirit have nothing, so whatever they gain is an improvement. Having nothing to lose, they are not proud and picky; having everything to gain, they are open, inventive, and frugal with what they receive. Little wonder God blesses them; they are so "blessable!"

On the other hand, the rich in spirit cannot be taught anything, for they already know it all. They have nothing to gain and everything to lose. Whatever comes along is either more of what they already have, or represents a threat which they fight off with their last ounce of strength.

There is a power in poverty of spirit — a freshness, a candor, an openness. Those who possess such simplicity of soul are very much like little children . . . and of such is the Kingdom of Heaven.

Yours,

*Phillips, p. 15.

35

Dear Friend,

Q: "Is there any question that cannot be truthfully answered 'Yes'?"

A: " 'Are you asleep?' is one such question."*

We recently had guests for dinner. The man ate heartily and, wanting to be a good host, I pushed more food on him. Finally he said, "No, thanks" and meant it. To make sure he was not just too embarrassed to ask for more, I questioned, "Are you absolutely sure you're not just being polite?" My question was idly phrased, but he picked up on it. "That's some corner you put me in: am I absolutely sure I'm not being polite?" To admit he was satisfied was one thing, but to admit he was not polite was another! He could not respond with a "Yes" to such a question.

Another such question comes to mind. It underlies what many people tell me when they come for counseling. They seem convinced that there is nothing they can do about their problem. Yet when I ask, "Are you sure there is nothing you can do about it?" they have to think carefully before they answer "Yes." That's quite an admission, that they are unable to take any action at all. I sometimes try tactfully to nudge them a little: "Let's go over your options. Are you absolutely sure there's nothing at all you can do?" "Well, not completely, I guess. I could pay back the money . . . or change my job . . . or move . . . or apologize . . ." It's hard to answer "Yes" truthfully to such a question.

Just as a sleeping person cannot practically answer "Yes" when asked if he's asleep; just as my guest could not graciously say "Yes" to his manners being lacking; even so a person in distress cannot say "Yes" when asked if he or she is totally without options.

Yours,

*Phillips, p. 16.

36

Dear Friend,

"If the iron is blunt, and one does not whet the edge, he must put forth more strength; but wisdom helps one to succeed. (Ecclesiastes 10:10)

We heat our summer camp with wood. Usually we buy it, but occasionally I do some chopping. I have a beautiful double-bitted ax, which I enjoy using. But it's hard to file it by hand, and even harder to find someone to sharpen it. So year by year it gets blunter, and I whack away more determinedly, with less satisfactory results. A little wisdom would help me a lot.

I'm sure each of you can think of a similar situation from your own personal experience. Do you keep on trying more of the same type of punishment for your child when the punishment you've tried has no effect? Do you keep arguing with your spouse over the same old, tired subjects, even though arguing never seems to bring about a resolution? Do you keep working harder to give your family everything it wants when what you've already given has not earned you their love and affection? It seems to be human nature to keep on repeating the same behavior we have tried before, and the more it doesn't work, the blunter our instrument becomes, the harder we have to strive for poorer results.

Jesus recognized this dilemma. He made the great call to salvation in this way: "Are you working hard and feeling heavier laden all the time? Then come to me; instead of your yoke, take my yoke. Learn of me. I know how things ought to go. Doing things my way, you will find rest for your souls." (paraphrase of Matthew 11:28, 29)

Yours,

37

Dear Friend,

Q: "I know the first half of a famous saying, but for the life of me, I can't remember the rest of it. Can you complete the sentence 'Where there's a will . . .'?"

A: "Where's there's a will, there is many an anxious relative."*

This little joke turns on the double meaning of the word "will." We are thinking "will power," and the author shocks us with "last will and testament."

There is all the difference in the world between "will and testament" and "will power." When the former is in effect, there is no more need for effort; when the latter is at work, all sorts of possibilities open to us.

Imagine this scene: a graduating senior in her "last will and testament" bequeaths to those who come after her her flattering ways which enabled her to just get by. Contrast this with the same young woman, faced with four more years of schooling, who decides, "I am going to buckle down and earn some decent grades." Her last will and testament is a declaration of what has been; her concentration of will power is a declaration of what can be.

Try this thought on for size: "At this point in my life if I were to make a bequest of what I've achieved, what would that heritage be?" Ah . . . er . . . ahem! So, it doesn't amount to much. Then switch "wills" to "will power." Lay out what you sincerely *will* do, today and all your tomorrows. Then you stand a very good chance of leaving behind a rich heritage indeed — so generous, in fact, that maybe even your relatives won't have to be anxious.

Yours,

*Phillips, p. 16.

38

Dear Friend,

Ecclesiastes has it, If the serpent bites before it is charmed, there is no advantage in a charmer. (10:11) A folk saying has it, "It's too late to lock the barn door after the horse has gone."

Expressions of wisdom join hands no matter their origin. The Bible derives its insights from divine inspiration and folk knowledge from centuries of experience. Our own personal experience bears witness to these truths: what a sad day it is indeed when we discover it is too late. "If only I had taken time to lock the barn door . . . to get to know my child . . . to study for that test . . . to accept Christ into my life . . . before it was too late."

A charmer who is busy making excuses, rather than tending to his serpent is paying mere lip-service to his work. A parent who does the same with a child is likewise insincere. To perceive the awe-inspiring truth in these sayings is to see our lives turned upside-down.

What is the deed you will wish you had done? Don't think about it, plan for it, or talk about it — *do it!* What is the relationship you know deep down is the most important one in your life? Don't substitute eloquence and excuses for vital, decisive action: *do it!* Do it, before the serpent strikes!

Yours,

39

Dear Friend,

Q: "I have been studying the Bible for years, but there is one question that I have not been able to get any answer to. Will you please tell me what kind of lights Noah used on his ark?"

A: "He must have used floodlights."*

We may also ask: "What kind of light did God use at Creation?" Genesis 1:3-5 tells us: *Daylight!* Since the beginning of time, day has signified the opposite of darkness. Life, warmth, understanding, even God himself are revealed to us through daylight.

Jesus lived fully in God's light and taught us how to share in it. Compared to God, we are tiny candles (Matthew 5:14-16). Yet, though only candles, we can still dispel the darkness. We are not to put our light under a bushel, but on a stand, so all may see in its glow.

What kind of light do we shed on others? *Growlight!* Perhaps you have one of these lights in your house or have seen one at a neighbor's. It gives a soft, comforting light, enabling seedlings to grow until, healthy and strong, they can be put out in the garden, to develop and thrive on their own.

Yours in dispelling darkness,

*Phillips, p. 13.

40

Dear Friend,

Q: "Why do ducks go into water?"

A: "For divers reasons, I guess."*

If we allow ducks to go into the water for "divers" reasons, why do we have so much trouble letting people do things "divers" ways?

Have you ever had a visitor from Europe who tells you in countless ways why they do it better in their country? Churches are often stopped dead in their tracks with the seven last words, "We have never done it that way." We lose friends and alienate family when we insist that others must do as we do.

If we can't let others do things their ways, whose problem is it, ours or theirs?

When people no longer entertain "divers" ways they become set in their ways and quickly turn to concrete. Stop expecting all ducks to go into the water the same way. Ponder the wonder and wealth of doing "divers" things in "divers" ways.

Yours,

*Phillips, p. 22.

41

Dear Friend,

Q: "What four-letter word do modern people find most objectionable?"

A: "Work."*

Something doesn't sit right with this joke. Is *work* really the most objectionable four-letter word? After all, there are *pain* and *fear* and *hate.* And it could be that *idle* is a far worse word than *work.*

These four-letter words have one thing in common. They involve isolation, or what can happen when we are cut off from others. We *hurt* alone, we *fear* alone, we *hate* alone, and when we are *idle,* we are most often alone.

But it's different with work. Work links us to others. To continue our four-letter theme: we *give* through work, we *make* things by working; we *earn* as we work and produce something to share, and we show that we *care* by our work. When we are at work, we are *busy* adding to the *good* things in *life.*

In fact, there is no way we can *show* that we *care* but by doing *work* of some kind. *Work* is the only way that *love,* in all its diverse expressions, can be shown to others.

I don't agree with this joke at all, even though it is meant to be just a bit of funny fluff. Only as we *work* do we become *part* of, and show that we *care* for the world around us.

Yours in labor and love,

*Phillips, p. 13.
(Suggested use: Labor Day)

42

Dear Friend,

A Tlingit Indian saying goes, "Teaching is like the mosquito. When the mosquito bites, you start itching. Even so, sometimes learning hurts." And we can add to that, "Sometimes learning itches."

Hurting or itching — learning affects us in different ways. At times it can be uncomfortable. It hurts to learn to admit when we are wrong and apologize in order to keep relationships from falling apart. It hurts to take the advice of another and learn to do things in a different way. It hurts to try harder when we think we can't summon up one more ounce of energy.

Learning also itches. Something tickles us deep inside, tempting us to scratch and get relief. We find relief by digging deeper into the issues than we might do otherwise. We get relief by laughing at our itch and trying new and more creative ways of "scratching." We find relief as we uncover the hidden meanings of the curious things that happen to us.

Ultimately, out of our hurting or itching, come better ways of doing things. So the next time things don't come easily to you, follow the example of the Tlingit Indians, and think upon the lowly mosquito.

Yours,

(Suggested use: Adult Education)

43

Dear Friend,

Oscar Wilde was a genius at hitting the nail on the head. He said, "There is no sin except stupidity." He joins with a classic definition that sin is to miss the mark. To know how to hit the mark is to be wise; not to know how to hit it and even to persist in missing it is to be and maybe insist on being stupid.

Wilde is worth listening to. The antidote to sin is to learn from those who know how to hit the mark. The Bible is a living record over hundreds of years of people who came to know how to hit the mark — to move from sin to salvation. If your life has been missing the mark, and you are ready for a new day, try learning from the experts: Moses, Joshua, Isaiah, Jeremiah, Amos, Matthew, Mark, Luke, John, and . . .

Yours,

(Suggested use: Adult Bible Study)

44

Dear Friend,

The title of my letter today is "The Forgotten Word." Look at Isaiah 9:6-7. He writes of the child who is to be born, that the government will be upon his shoulder; of the increase of this government there will be no end. He will ". . . establish it, and to uphold it with justice and with righteousness. . ."

Where is peace as the foundation of his government? It is the forgotten word. We can well ask why Isaiah did not list peace as the foundation of his government along with justice and righteousness? I found out why from a bumper sticker. *If you want peace fight for justice.* Peace is the result of justice and righteousness, not their cause. We do not experience justice because we are peaceful. We enjoy peace because we are just.

Peace is not the cause of anything; it is the end of diligence and wisdom, vigilance and courage. Look sometimes and see how much Scripture is devoted to justice. God is a God of love *and* justice. The words are almost synonymous. When we are called to seek peace and pursue it — we are actually being called to lives of justice and righteousness. Only then can peace dwell secure in the land.

Yours,

(Suggested use: World Order Sunday)

45

Dear Friend,

Q: "Can you give me some examples of a collective noun?"

A: "Three collective nouns come to mind right away — flypaper, wastepaper basket, and vacuum cleaner."*

That time of year has come around again when we need to talk about collective nouns like the offering plate, the pledge card and envelope, and special offerings.

Some churches (sometimes even our own!) operate like flypaper. Every time members come to church, they get "stuck." Others are like wastepaper baskets: the church officials figure people have money to throw away — ask, ask, ask, without any serious accounting. Finally, some churches are like vacuum cleaners, sucking up all they can get. I remember a preacher taking up a major collection. He started with the "silent" offering — only bills, big bills! Then a "silent" offering of little bills. Finally, he called for a "sound" offering — he wanted to hear all those coins jingle in the plate!

We at _______ Church do not choose to function in these ways. Certainly we are a collective institution, or we could not exist. But we are not flypaper: we ask only for a responsible act of stewardship at the time of the canvass and then faithfulness to it during the year. We are not a wastepaper basket: we make a responsible accounting of the genuine needs for the year, with a valid margin for growth. And we are not a vacuum cleaner. We feel acting in this manner insults your integrity.

Let's collect all we can, in a stewardshiplike manner, and serve the collective cause of Christ as devoutly as we may.

Yours,

*Phillips, p. 17.
(Suggested use: Annual Canvass)

46

Dear Friend,

Jewish astrological tradition connects the appearance of the Messiah with the conjunction of Jupiter and Saturn that occurs in Pisces. Pisces was regarded as the constellation of the Jews, and Saturn was the planet of the Jews because of its association with Saturday, the Sabbath, and because it was "most high," the most distant planet known to the ancients. Hence it was a manifestation of the Most High God.

Jupiter was the star of the Messiah, because its conjunction with Saturn symbolized the transfer of power from the Most High God to his Messianic King. So when the wise men saw "his star in the East" (Matthew 2:2), they were probably observing Jupiter. In Hebrew the planet's name is "sedheq," meaning "justice," or "vindication," words often associated with the Messiah.

Just a bit of relevant folklore I thought you might like to ponder as we enter this holy advent season.

Yours,

(Suggested use: Advent)

47

Dear Friend,

When we go to a large theater and sit waiting for the curtain to rise on whatever lies ahead for the evening, we are caught up in excitement. What images fill the mind! What will the action be, the set, the cast of characters? The orchestra strikes up the overture, the lights go down, a hush comes over the audience. Slowly, the curtain begins to rise . . .

That's how I feel during Advent season. I'm sitting in a vast theater — vast as the globe, vast as the universe — waiting for the curtain to rise. I have had a sneak preview of the set and know some of the actors, but what about the drama? Whatever it may be, it is greater than any human drama, for it is the fulfillment of God's promise to humankind, and it has been centuries in the making. And, it is the divine playwright himself who is behind the scenes, directing events.

The overture is over, the lights go down, a hush settles . . .

Yours, in anticipation,

(Suggested use: Advent)

48

Dear Friend,

All of us have sometimes had the opportunity to listen to bright, clever people. They are much in demand; they test well, make high grades, demonstrate technical proficiency. They are the "brains" of society, the ones that the world envies and rewards.

There is another dimension to intelligence, and it goes beyond being bright and clever. In fact, being bright and clever may get in the way, because the clever individual will consider nothing which cannot be analyzed or fed into a computer system. This other dimension of intelligence we call "wisdom."

Every Christmas season we talk about the Three Wise Men, who could read astrological signs and make important deductions. They were bright and clever, but they were also something else. They were able to set aside reliance on their own knowledge and journey on to discover mysteries beyond their mortal intelligence — and that is what made them wise men. On our life journeys, practical knowledge is useful and necessary, but surrendering ourselves up to God's higher designs is the beginning of divine wisdom. Happy journeying this Christmastide.

Yours,

(Suggested use: Fourth Sunday in Advent)

49

Dear Friend,

Q: "I have been experimenting with different ways of making fire. Can you tell me if there is an easy way to start a fire by using just two pieces of wood?"

A: "It is easy to start a fire with two pieces of wood if one of those pieces of wood is a match."*

You are at a meeting and you keep thinking, "Why don't 'they' get down to work and do something? Where's the fire in this group?" Try being a match.

You are sitting in church thinking that the pastor is a wooden-head and ought to be doing this and that. If only he could get it all together and start a fire in the congregation! Try being a match.

You are at home, thinking wistfully of your mate, "If only he — or she — were more loving, our marriage would really catch fire." Try being a match.

At work, you wish the boss would exert more leadership, that your co-workers would put more muscle into their efforts. Be a match!

In your community, if only the leaders were more concerned, the citizens more committed. Be a match!

In the year ahead, the next time you fret about the waste of time, talent, and vitality, and you wonder why nothing seems to be on fire . . . anytime . . . any place. Be a match!

Yours, for lighting up the New Year,

*Phillips, p. 21.
(Suggested use: New Year's)

50

Dear Friend,

Comedian Bob Hope once reported a snow storm in Palm Springs. He called it "God's way of reminding the rich that he is more powerful than they are."

I feel that way about the sun — massive cosmic forces at work to bring the sunshine in my window, forces far beyond the control of humankind. The whole movement of the earth and sun puts into relief our utter reliance on God's ways.

The word "Lent" comes from the Old English "lencten." Its meaning matches the way it sounds: "lengthen." I find it very satisfying to monitor the sun as the days lengthen in the spring. A few weeks ago I was eating breakfast in the haze of sunrise; now I do so in bright sunlight. That says something to me. It reminds me of God's sovereign power over his creation, that there is a predictability about the days and the seasons. At this special time of year, I take great comfort in that fact.

Yours,

(Suggested use: Lent)

51

Dear Friend,

A logical connection between "as" and "even so" runs through the Scripture, and from Scripture into our lives. "*As* the father sent me, *even so* I send you. *As* I breathe upon you and give the Holy Spirit, *even so* you are to breathe your influence into the lives of others and pass it along. *As* Thomas was reluctant to believe until he saw, *even so* we are reluctant. *As* those who believe without seeing are blessed, *even so* we are blessed when we believe without seeing. *As* others have experienced the Christ in Jesus, *even so* do we."

A great deal can be communicated through such parallelisms. *As* the tension inherent in the resurrection permeated all events for the disciples and helped build the early church, *even so* the resurrection permeates events for us this Eastertide and helps build the church. After all, every Sunday throughout the year is a little Easter. *As* we relive the events of the gospel story, *even so* a creative tension enters our lives as we enter into fellowship with Christ.

The language need not be so elevated. At the heart of the matter is a very simple concept: *As* people have seen and borne witness to Jesus down through the centuries, even so do we today. *As* the living Christ empowered people in the gospel events, *even so* he frees us from self-imposed limitations and puts us to Kingdom work.

Yours,

(Suggested use: Pentecost)

52

Dear Friend,

We have shared this year together in many ways, and now the time has come for many of us to part as we go our vacation ways. A benediction is fitting. I choose one from Philippians 4:20 — "To our God and Father be glory forever and ever. Amen."

All that has been experienced and accomplished during the past year is meant for one purpose only: to bring glory to God.

All we have been in our relationships — whatever was required of us in the way of faithfulness, support, love, and upbuilding — all this was meant for one ultimate purpose: to reflect the greatness of the grace of God.

All our works, the way we used our talents, the intentions we invested in action, the careful workmanship we gave to the jobs assigned us — all this for one reason only: to demonstrate to others the quality of our reverence for God.

All our giving, the money we shared, the works it made possible, our gratefulness for the opportunity to give, the tug in our hearts inspired by Christ's compassion for the world — for one purpose only: that God's works begun here might continue and thrive always.

So, as we go our separate ways, all we have been and done together rises like an anthem of praise to add to the glory of God at work in the world, and to proclaim to the world that, as we have lived together in peace, cooperation, and love, we are all children of one Father.

Amen,

(Suggested use: Before Vacation Sundays)

Postscript

Dear Friend,

We have spent a month of Mondays together. During this time we have looked at the Gospel in as many ways. In each of these we celebrated Christ's power to remove barriers, lift spirits, alter destructive courses, and empower faint hearts into productivity.

We have sought to stretch minds upward to the wisdom of Christ; to reach out and out, touching others as effectively as our intention and skill allow; and to explore the deep mysteries of ourselves as we relate to Christ our Lord.

Too often we pastors are encased in what is immediately before us — the daily demands of good administration, service to the bureaucracy, doing what we think people and superiors think we should do, and chastising ourselves when it doesn't all work together.

We have to remember our vital resource. Christ's meaning is not exhausted even if we fulfill all these demands. He stands before us and holds out that which is yet possible, beyond our predictions, plannings, and expectations. That's why he is good news.

We have yet another major resource, the personal and professional support we and we alone can give each other. In a unique way we support each other. We lift the sights of other pastors by the way we apprehend the best in them. Our empathic responses to our brothers and sisters expands the supportive arms of Christ. And, our integrity of relationships calls forth that which lies yet-unexplored in the depths of our selves. No matter the cost to ourselves and the bureaucracy of the church, care for each other is a prime responsibility and can be done by us alone.

Yours,

Thomas D. Peterson